SUCCESSF

INTERVIEW

Mike Levy

60 Minutes Success Skills Series

Copyright © David Grant Publishing Limited 1998

First published 1998 by
David Grant Publishing Limited
80 Ridgeway, Pembury, Kent TN2 4EZ United Kingdom

99   98   10 9 8 7 6 5 4 3 2 1

60 Minutes Success Skills Series is an imprint of
David Grant Publishing Limited

British Library Cataloguing in Publication Data
A CIP record for this book is available from the British Library

ISBN 1-901306-11-9

Cover design: Steve Haynes
Text design: Graham Rich
Production Editor: Paul Stringer
Typeset in Futura
by Archetype IT Ltd, web site http://www.archetype-it.com

Printed and bound in Great Britain by
T.J. International, Padstow, Cornwall

This book is printed on acid-free paper

CONTENTS

ABOUT *SUCCESSFUL INTERVIEWING*

Can you learn to get to grips with interviewing skills in one hour? The answer is a resounding "Yes".

The 60 Minutes Success Skills series is written for people with neither the time nor the patience to trawl through acres of jargon, management-speak and page-filling waffle. Like all the books in the series, it has been written in the belief that you can learn all you really need to know quickly and without hassle. The aim is to distil the essential, practical advice you can use straight away. Let's get to work.

Is this book for you?

Successful Interviewing is packed full of useful and practical advice for the would-be ace recruiter. In today's competitive labour markets, it is vital to make sure you have the right person for the right job. The crux of any recruitment procedure, however sophisticated, is the face-to-face interview. It can be a nerve-wracking time for both parties. How do you decide? How can you be sure you've made the best choice of person? Have you been fair and given the interviewee every opportunity?

This book is also very useful for people being interviewed. Interviewing is all about technique – asking the right questions and being ready to give the best answers. If you want to improve your interviewing skills, or want to do better at interviews, this book is definitely for you.

If your interviewing skills need a quick pep-me-up then this quick, no-bull guide is just what you need. Read on.

How to use this book

The message here is "It's OK to skim". Feel free to flick through to find the help you most need. This book is a collection of hands-on tips which will help you to spot any shortcomings you might have and show you how to turn them into strengths. You **can** become the slick interviewer you've always wanted to be.

Successful Interviewing has been written to dip into. You don't have to read it all at one go or follow every tip to the letter. If you're really pushed for time, you could skip through the book following the boxed features. These summarise each of the points covered by prompting you to think about an issue, and then giving you action points which are backed up with lists of handy tips to keep you on the right track.

GOOD LUCK!

The author

Mike Levy is a freelance business journalist, author, trainer and grants consultant. His training courses include interviewing skills, marketing, customer care, stress management and EU funding.
For more details contact: mike@levy-writer.demon.co.uk

What's in this chapter for you

> *The importance of getting it right*
> *The nightmare interview*
> *Why use the interview?*
> *The perfect interviewer*

"All the jobs in our company are subject to an interview.
It's the way it's always been done! I couldn't appoint anyone
without an interview, however good they look on paper – it's the
human touch that counts. Is there any other way? **"**
                               – Don Cole, personnel officer

The importance of getting it right

Does Don's attitude sound familiar? It should: Almost every new
job in the country is filled as the result of a successful interview.

> When was the last time you conducted an interview? Did you
> get the right person for the job? When was the last time you
> were interviewed? Did they get the correct impression of you?

"*I'm terrible at giving interviews. I get as flustered as the
candidates and only think of the best questions after they've gone.* **"**
                               – Jon Wagstaff, wine warehouse owner

Interviewing has become the most common method of
recruitment selection. However, there is a question mark over the
usefulness of interviews. It is not certain how good they are at
predicting the eventual performance of a candidate. We have all
experienced interviews that have gone really badly, where we
might say, "They really didn't get to know me" or "They seemed
to have decided before the interview even began". These are all
signs not of the weakness of the interview itself, but of a poorly
planned and executed session. Interviews can be very powerful
predictors – but they need to be done properly. Done badly they
can be worse than useless – a waste of people's time and money.

> **❝**We spend all day interviewing candidates for a job. It involves the principal, the head of studies, the senior teacher and a governor. When you add up what it costs in staff time, not to mention the work lost for that day, it doesn't bear thinking about. We are actively looking for a better way to recruit new staff **❞**.
> – **Pam Henderson, primary head teacher**

Pam's experience is not untypical. Interviews are costly and not always guaranteed to work. As predictors of likely job competence, they have proved to be poor (often ranking only slightly higher than pure guesswork and astrology!).

The nightmare interview

Interviews can and do go wrong. Bad interviews can leave interviewees feeling embittered and damage their self-esteem. For an organisation it's just as damaging to have a "good" interview which picks the "wrong" person.

> **❝**It's quite common here for people to do really well at interview, only to prove that they don't come up to scratch in the job. One chap we employed as a department manager, who had interviewed really well, turned out to have dire people management skills. It cost us two of our best junior account managers and morale has still not been restored. **❞**
> – **Lisa Perrot, financial services company**

Think about the consequences of a nightmare interview for you or your organisation. It goes deeper than just the loss of time and money in the short term – there's also your reputation at stake. This is why it's vital to avoid the pitfalls.

Here are some reasons why interviews go wrong.

○ *The wrong type of interview has been used. There's more than one way to interview a candidate. One person, face-to-face may be the least effective (see the next chapter).*
○ *The interview has been badly planned. The secret of good interviews lies in the planning: knowing what to ask and why; knowing how to interpret the responses.*
○ *An inexperienced (or incompetent) interviewer.*

The Un-Magnificent Seven

The skills of the interviewer are key to getting it right so ensure you assess whoever is conducting any interviews in your organisation and look at possible training needs.

Here are seven sure-fire signs of interviewer incompetence. If you spot these in yourself or others, do your best to put them right. They are all to be avoided. The interviewer:

- ❏ *wants to do all the talking*
- ❏ *is a very poor listener (and shows it)*
- ❏ *is very disorganised (can't find the application form, doesn't know who the interviewee is, hasn't arranged a venue for the interview)*
- ❏ *has his or her mind made up before a word is spoken*
- ❏ *allows interruptions from outside*
- ❏ *can't be heard – mumbles or mutters*
- ❏ *asks too many "closed" questions (one's where only "yes" or "no" is required) and doesn't give the respondent a chance to elaborate (more on this in chapter five).*

Remember: It is vitally important to get the right person for the job. Just keep thinking that the consequences of choosing the wrong person are:

- ○ *Lost orders or production*
- ○ *Damage to the team working aspects of your organisation*
- ○ *Dissatisfied customers*
- ○ *Increased costs.*

Why use the interview?

It may seem like a silly question but you need to be sure that you are using the interview for the best reasons (and not just out of habit).

❝*We have a six monthly staff assessment which takes the form of an interview with a line manager. Frankly, it's not something that either side looks forward to. I often wonder if we could do it a different way.* ❞
– Wes Holder, MD of a packing company

There are many good reasons for using a well-planned interview. What we're saying here is simply that you should look at alternatives where they exist.

> Have you ever wondered why you use the interview method? Ask yourself if you're sure it's the best way to pick new staff, carry out an appraisal and so on. Make sure you can answer fully the questions below each time you want to hold an interview.

Whenever you plan to use an interview, ask yourself these two questions:

○ *(1) What is the interview actually for – i.e. what are its objectives? These may include:*
  – *to find the best person for the job*
  – *to check the details sent on a CV or application form*
  – *to get a personal impression of the person*
  – *to see whether the person is likely to fit into your team*
  – *to confirm you can really work together*
  – *to check their general fitness for the job or task*
  – *to assess the likely potential of the candidate*
  – *to provide the candidate with the information he or she needs (remember that interviewing is a two-way process)*
  – *to really test the candidate's mettle.*
○ *(2) Are there any alternatives to the formal face-to-face interview? You should always consider using:*
  – *psychometric tests*
  – *questionnaires to screen the candidates*
  – *panel interviews*
  – *assessment days, during which the candidate's ability and potential is measured over time and perhaps in the work place*
  – *other forms of "scientific" testing.*

(See the next chapter for more on the alternatives.)

"We've replaced the old-fashioned one-to-one interview by asking our short-listed candidates to go on a two-day assessment at our country centre. This involves them working in a team, trying their hand at problem solving, working with existing employees and managers. This kind of "on the job"*

assessment works really well for us. It has proved to be a very good predictor of people's potential. **"**
– Marc Levitt, CEO of a drug research company

Are you able to develop an assessment procedure? Do you have the resources, staff and time to do this? Even if you do, the formal interview may still be really useful as a way to sift out the weaker candidates and provide a "first round" initial assessment.

The perfect interviewer

What is a successful interview? How do you know when you have become a successful interviewer? Everyone needs some kind of benchmark against which to judge their competence.

It's true to say: "Great interviewers are rarely born, they are usually made." Here are some characteristics of the competent interviewer. By remembering these and trying to copy as many as you can, you'll be sure to improve your own technique.

The good interviewer:

- ❑ *Gives the candidate enough time to put his or her strengths across*
- ❑ *Chooses the right venue – where the surroundings help to put the interviewee at ease*
- ❑ *Has a clear idea about the job specification – and knows it without having to read through notes during the session*
- ❑ *Knows the job or tasks that the successful interviewee may have to carry out*
- ❑ *Has read the candidate's CV or application form thoroughly and knows a lot about him or her before the interview*
- ❑ *Establishes a good rapport with the interviewee so that proper discussion can take place*
- ❑ *Guides the discussion or conversation, but never takes over*
- ❑ *Is a very good listener*
- ❑ *Has prepared a strategy for asking the right questions at the right time*
- ❑ *Ignores anything said which is irrelevant to the job in hand*
- ❑ *Makes a clear written record of what the candidate said, how he or she behaved and what impressions were gathered.*

*" I've become really good at interviewing. I seem to able
to get the best from the interviewees and find out exactly what I need
to pick the right person for the job – I suppose it's a skill. I've
certainly not recently compromised the effectiveness of
my team by appointing a dork! "*
– Danny Webster, industrial team leader

By the end of this book you should be well on your way to
achieving "perfect interviewer" status.

Ten first steps towards Successful Interviewing

1. Think about your current interviewing policy. Is it working well or can you see flaws?
2. Start a discussion in your organisation to see if current interview practice can be improved.
3. When it comes to job selection and recruitment, don't assume that one-to-one interviews are 100% reliable and that you should use one-to-ones simply because "that's the way it's always been done".
4. Take into account the costs of your current interview system in terms of staff time and resources. Can the expenditure be justified?
5. Learn by heart the "Un-Magnificent 7" traits of a poor interviewer. This will tell you what you must stop doing if you find yourself guilty of them.
6. Think about some of the alternatives to interviewing. Are they appropriate?
7. Make sure that every interview is well prepared and has a clear set of objectives.
8. Do your homework – make sure you know a lot about the candidate and the job to be filled before the interview.
9. Get the setting right – not too formal but avoiding the over-casual.
10. Look again at the criteria for the perfect interviewer – make a list of the attributes you want to possess. Put these into a rank order of importance for you. In other words, set your own high standards.

What's in this chapter for you

Face-to-face, one-to-one interviews
Group interviews
Serial interviews
Problem-solving and role-play interviews
Daring to be different
The pre-interview – using the telephone
Appraisal and disciplinary interviews

> ❝ *I know it has its faults, but we feel that the face-to-face interview is the best way to assess the likely future performance of a candidate. I mean, how else can you tell?* ❞
> **– Reg Wilkes, head of a carpet store**

Types of interview

"Surely an interview is an interview!" No. Interviews come in many varieties, as we will see. The traditional face-to-face, one-to-one selection interview is still the most common form, but it is by no means always the most effective. This issue provokes some very different reactions.

> ❝ *As personnel manager, I think it's my job to interview a candidate. Occasionally I might bring in a colleague with specialist knowledge – but that's rare. After all, I am the recruitment specialist.* ❞
> **– Anne Gould**

> ❝ *My belief is that a new recruit to our business must be a first-class team worker. It's only fair to let the existing team have some say in new appointments. We try to include representatives across the organisation in selection interviews.* ❞
> **– Bryn Williams, head of an engineering firm**

Have you got an open mind about the type of interview you should conduct? You should – the alternatives offer interesting possibilities.

We can distinguish four different types of interview:

○ *One-to-one interview – still the most common type.*
○ *Group interview – where two or more interviewers are present.*
○ *Serial interviews – where a candidate is asked to attend two or more consecutive interviews.*
○ *Problem-solving and role-play interviews – where candidates have to demonstrate their abilities.*

The picture gets more complicated because interviews can also be held for different reasons:

○ *Job selection*
○ *Appraisal*
○ *Disciplinary*
○ *Screening*
○ *Exit*

Let's look at the different types of interview in turn.

One-to-one interviews

❝ *This is the way we've always done it. As the personnel manager, it's my job to face the candidate – just him or her, and me. That's the way I like it. It's my responsibility.* ❞
– Anne Gould

The "one to one" is the most traditional form of interview. It's what most people expect and it has a long tradition. Many people got their first and subsequent jobs from one-to-one interviews – it's a known quantity. One-to-one interviews come in different forms.

The "informal chat"

In these, the setting and the tone of the interview are designed to put the candidate at ease. It's a chance to find out more about the person by seeing them "as they really are". The trouble is, that interviewers are not always convincingly "informal".

Do you agree with this? "I hate informal interviews. I like to know where I stand. There's nothing more nerve wracking than an interviewer trying hard to be relaxed!"

More formal but unstructured

The problem with the unstructured interview is one of inconsistency. For instance, with unplanned interviews, it is very easy to forget to ask all of the candidates the most vital questions. This problem is quite common.

Do you agree with this from a fairly experienced interviewer? "Of course I do a bit of homework about the candidate, but I like to let the interview develop its own momentum – I don't like to be tied down to a rigid structure. Let the discussion flow is my motto."

On the whole, unstructured interviews (where you make up the questions as you go along) have a tendency to be:

○ *either too long or too short*
○ *unfair in that they treat people in different ways*
○ *too reliant on mood, circumstance and chance.*

Structured and fully planned

Fundamentally, these involve asking all candidates the same (or similar questions) so that at least there is some consistency. See chapter five for more advice but remember: the better prepared your interview, the better will be the outcome.

> ❝ *It's tiring at first but saves a lot of time and energy in the end. I always spend at least as long in preparing the interview as I do in carrying it out!* ❞
> **– Bob Munro, director of a canning factory**

Done well, one-to-one interviews can be very effective. Let's look at some strengths and weaknesses of this form of interview.

Strengths:

- ○ *Chance to build a rapport quickly*
- ○ *Easier to relate to people on this basis*
- ○ *It is what is usually expected.*

Weaknesses:

- ○ *It can be very stressful for both parties*
- ○ *As an interviewer, you have no one with whom to discuss the merits (or otherwise) of the candidates*
- ○ *It can be very tiring for the interviewer*

Group interviews

These involve anything from two to fifteen (or even more) interviewers in a panel.

> ❝ *We usually have a panel of three interviewers – my works supervisor, the floor manager and myself. We work out roughly in advance what we are going to ask and what we're looking for in a person. I like the format because the selection is a team effort rather than a one-man decision.* ❞
> **– Marc Levitt**

Group interviews are increasingly common. They provide a team approach to interviewing that many people find useful.

Strengths:

- ○ *Different interviewers can specialise in certain fields of questioning – one might concentrate, for example, on technical matters, another on personal development, team building and so on*
- ○ *Interviewers can be drawn from a wide cross-section of the organisation*
- ○ *Interviewers or "observers" can help in the final selection process – many heads are better than one*
- ○ *It gives colleagues a say in selection procedure*

Weaknesses:

- ○ *It can be more stressful for the interviewees to face a panel of people*
- ○ *Time might be wasted in unnecessary discussion and argument*
- ○ *It may be more difficult to manage and structure the interview the way you want it to go.*

" We moved over to group interviews two years ago. Instead of me or a colleague having to face the nervous interviewees eyeball to eyeball, we formed groups of four or five interviewers drawn from different parts of the business. It was chaos at first. We spent a lot of time asking the same question, some colleagues talked too much and there was hardly ever any agreement on how, let alone who, to select for the job. We quickly learnt that group interviews need to be carefully organised. "
– Alan Mullery, grocery wholesalers' personnel manager

Alan's experience is fairly common. Group interviews can go badly wrong unless there are clear and strict criteria for running the session. See chapter five for more on this.

Serial interviews

With this type of interview, candidates are asked to attend several sessions over a period of time.

Have you ever attended a series of interviews (where there are several rounds)? What did you think? Do you prefer them to the one-off interview?

Strengths:

○ *This form can combine the advantages of the group with the one-to-one interview. Each interview can be conducted by a specialist manager.*
○ *It's less of a "sudden death" experience for interviewees. They have a second chance to shine.*
○ *You can get to know more about the candidate. Some people find it easier to go to several interviews and are consequently more natural.*
○ *The sequence of interviews can also be used to whittle down a long list of candidates – unsuccessful interviewees drop out at each successive stage.*
○ *A series of sessions can include worthwhile problem-solving exercises.*

Weaknesses:

○ *The process can lose momentum*
○ *If taken over too long a time, it may be difficult to come to a decision*
○ *It can be costly (especially if your organisation is paying the expenses of the interviewees).*

Problem-solving and role-play interviews

In these interviews, candidates can be given "real-life" exercises or simulations that will test their abilities and confirm they have the skills that will be needed in the job.

Such active interview sessions are becoming more common, especially for middle and senior management posts. Candidates may be asked to perform an "in-tray exercise". That means dealing with typical issues that they may have to face. The in-tray may consist of several "memos", reports, action plans, diary notes that have to be acted upon etc. These and similar exercises are used to test the candidate's ability to:

○ *prioritise*
○ *organise the workload*
○ *solve problems*
○ *deal with people-related issues*
○ *communicate with others*
○ *concentrate under pressure.*

Strengths:

○ *Given that some candidates are very good at being interviewees (and others particularly bad), these sessions are a more instructive way of testing their abilities to do the job rather than their interview skills.*
○ *You have the chance to actually observe the candidate under real "work" conditions.*

Weaknesses:

○ *Simulations and role-play exercises can be unrealistic*
○ *These exercises cannot fully replicate good team working*
○ *Many candidates find these exercises to be very stressful.*

These kinds of interview are best carried out in special "assessment centres".

Daring to be different

The main thing to realise about interviews is that there's often more than one option. Look at different ways of conducting them. Consider using group, serial or problem-solving interviews rather than the traditional face-to-face which can be an ordeal for both parties.

Re-assess the way your organisation carries out selection interviews. Is there a different and better way to conduct them? Look at the strengths and weaknesses of the different types of interview. How might they work in your organisation?

The pre-interview stage – using the telephone

" *I often find that most of the useful work when selecting people is done over the phone.* "
– **Kate McDonald, MD of a publishing house**

Think back to a time when someone called you on the telephone about a job (or you did the telephoning). What first impressions did you get or give? Did it help or hinder in getting the job?

Selection interviews are all about discovering the talents, potential and personality of the candidate. You can be as objective as you like, but we should never underestimate the influence of first impressions. A telephone call is often the first we hear from a prospective employee. They may be asking for more information about the vacancy or responding to a request to have an informal chat before proceeding with the application.

" *In our recruitment advertisements, I always put "Ring Carole for further information about this post". That way I can suss out if a candidate is really qualified for the position, and it also gives me a*

chance to gather some initial impressions. Of course, we can't rely on a short telephone call, but it can say a lot about a person. **"**
– Carole Cockburn, personnel officer
in a mobile phone company

> How confident are you on the telephone? Do you think a phone conversation is a reliable way of gauging the potential of a candidate?

Just as there are communication skills which make us good or bad on the telephone, there are listening skills which enable us to pick up useful clues about a person's abilities, interests, skills and potential. We will explore more on listening skills in chapter four. For now, consider using the telephone as a useful, but incomplete, source of gathering first impressions. These impressions should always be backed up by meeting the person – there really is no substitute for this.

> Telephone interviews are useful for:
>
> ❏ *Establishing the basic facts – has the candidate got the minimum requirements and qualifications? It is a useful screening tool which can save management time and resources.*
> ❏ *Starting to build a rapport that can be further built upon in the "live" meeting.*
> ❏ *Testing the ability of the candidate to communicate (if this is indeed an important quality required).*
> ❏ *Ensuring that the candidate comes to the live interview with the correct documents, at the right place and time.*

The message here is to consider using telephone interviews as a preliminary screening device and a way of preparing candidates for the live session. Here are some useful do's and don'ts of telephone interviewing.

○ **DON'T:**
  – *Try to catch the candidate off guard. It doesn't serve your interests to have the person nervous and unprepared.*
  – *Try to explain complex organisational or technical issues that are best left to the face-to-face meeting.*
  – *Do all the talking. The point of telephoning the candidate is to find out about him or her.*
  – *Waste time with too many niceties and irrelevant chat.*
  – *Make the telephone call if you're not a good "phone person". Leave it to others.*
  – *Offer the job on the basis of a telephone call.*
○ **DO:**
  – *Concentrate on listening properly (see chapter four).*
  – *Set up a time convenient to both parties, when the interview can take place.*
  – *Take notes so that you have a record of the conversation and make sure all necessary details are given.*
  – *Speak in a calm, slow, confident voice that aims to put the interviewee at ease.*
  – *Use your questioning skills (see chapter six) – try to draw out what the interviewee is thinking.*
  – *Be polite.*

Appraisal and disciplinary interviews

Although this book is primarily concerned with selection interviews, there are other equally important types. Appraisal interviews, for instance, have become increasingly common in the last few years. These can be quite difficult to conduct because:

○ *you may be dealing with quite close colleagues – some organisations even involve upward appraisal where you appraise your line manager*
○ *you may have to bring up personal problems and shortcomings*
○ *you may have to discuss past failures as well as successes*
○ *appraisees often see these as public criticism sessions, so the level of stress is often very high*
○ *appraisers are often worried over thinking of ways to motivate staff.*

Have you ever attended or conducted an appraisal interview? How well did it go? Can you think of ways in which it could have been improved?

Appraisals should be on-going processes but if this not the case things which have been bottled up for months may come out during the interview. This can make the session even more stressful.

> **Follow these useful guidelines to help you run a reduced-stress appraisal interview:**
>
> ❑ *Make sure that you know exactly what you have to do: the more confident you are, the better the session will go.*
> ❑ *Put the interviewee at ease straight away. Start with some informal small talk.*
> ❑ *Make the room as comfortable and relaxing as possible and don't allow any outside interruptions.*
> ❑ *Keep the discussion fairly formal but try to maintain a friendly atmosphere.*
> ❑ *Remember that the main point of the appraisal is to let the interviewee do most of the talking.*
> ❑ *Reassure the person that this is not a disciplinary interview (it's amazing how often the two are confused).*
> ❑ *Never stoop to using bullying tactics.*

Remember: the main point of the interview is to assess the *performance* of the interviewee, not air any personal hang-ups you have about their conduct or habits. Praise any successes and perceived strengths before going on to diagnose any problems or weaknesses. Allow the interviewee to comment on any appraisal criteria used – are they fair, consistent and accurate? Can they be improved?

If needs be, suggest ways of overcoming any shortcomings and help formulate an action plan. Then set up a mutually acceptable monitoring process to keep a check on progress.

> **Remember to ask the interviewee for his or her views on strengths and weaknesses. Don't confront interviewees with accusations about performance. It is far better to let them identify these weaknesses themselves. Your job is to guide them towards this self-awareness.**

❝ *It's much better to ask: "So, what are the areas that could be improved upon? Is there anything you've done in the last year that, with hindsight, you could have done more effectively?" than "Why did you make such a mess of the project?" If you get the appraisees to set the improvement agenda, there's a much better chance of making genuine progress.* ❞
– Graham Taylor, training consultant

Never forget that: "Appraisal interviews are all about Leading and Feeding not Bleating and Beating."

Try to get to the bottom of any problems. Don't put them down to personal weaknesses. This won't get you anywhere: it will create an upset, dispirited and demotivated employee. Analyse each fault carefully and find the cause:

- ❑ *Is it lack of training? If so, establish the training needs and book the interviewee on any relevant courses.*
- ❑ *Is it lack of organisation? Point the appraisee towards a more time-efficient way of working if it is.*
- ❑ *Is it lack of motivation? What is the root of the problem here? It could be more to do with personal life than the job. Find out sympathetically and suggest ways forward.*

You cannot and should not shame the interviewee into doing better. Your job as appraiser is to suggest ways of overcoming problems and weaknesses. It's about realistic target setting and, above all, motivating your staff.

How good are you at appraising others? Are you objective? Do you let your prejudices and interest get in the way of sound and impartial judgement?

❝ *We run appraisal interviews in small teams, although the appraisee only sees one person at a time. The benefit is that you can discuss the merits of each case. It's all too easy to misjudge people. I really appreciate having this team approach.* ❞
– May Daniels, director of a small souvenir company

Disciplinary interviews

Disciplinary interviews, especially where dismissal is likely, can be hard to face. Yet, in these, there is more reason than ever to be as professional an interviewer as possible. There is a lot at stake: the future of the employee, relations within departments, staff morale in general, pressures from unions and other interested parties.

> **❝** *I dread disciplinary interviews. I know it's part of my job but I find them embarrassing, upsetting and difficult to face.* **❞**
> **– May Daniels**

Here are a few golden rules for running professional disciplinary interviews

- ❑ *Keep the tone formal but make it clear that you are still approachable.*
- ❑ *Stick rigidly to the organisation's disciplinary code and procedures – never make up the rules as you go along.*
- ❑ *Be aware of any employment legislation that sets out rights and responsibilities. Make sure you know all the acceptable sanctions that can be applied, from a warning to dismissal.*
- ❑ *Thoroughly investigate the facts of the case and get them straight before the interview.*
- ❑ *Talk to witnesses or others central to the case and check on the interviewee's work record.*
- ❑ *Allow the interviewee to make his or her position clear in advance of the hearing.*
- ❑ *Keep a detailed record of what was said or promised in the interview so you can explain the final decision carefully and fully (usually in writing).*

To put this "ordeal" in perspective, consider the likely outcomes – play around with "what if?" scenarios. For instance, what if:

- ○ *the breach of discipline has few repercussions?*
- ○ *the evidence against him or her won't stand up to scrutiny?*
- ○ *this is a first offence or something out of character?*
- ○ *there is some kind of reason for the bad behaviour?*
- ○ *you formally warn the person?*
- ○ *you dismiss the person?*

What we have said about selection interviews can also apply to appraisal interviews and disciplinary hearings. Consider whether the traditional one-to-one interview is the best form.

Top tips on interview types

1. Look critically at your interviewing methods. Which one do you normally use and why? Is it delivering the results you want?

2. Do your homework. It's crucial to use your selection interview to achieve set objectives – this means you should know exactly what the job involves and how critically you need to assess the candidates. A single one-to-one interview will probably be sufficient for the job of assistant deputy stationery monitor whereas you might need a series of group interviews in combination with problem-solving and role-play assessment to recruit a high-level project manager.

3. Don't stick with tradition. Consider the strengths and weaknesses of the group or panel interview and do the same for problem-solving or role-play exercises. And don't be scared to use them as part of your interview regime.

4. Try to avoid unstructured interviews. They might be good for relaxing interviewees, but you will almost certainly slip into the trap of being inconsistent in the questions you ask and perhaps even forget some of the most important ones.

5. Use the telephone pre-interview to do the factual background check on the candidate. This will also allow you to begin to build up a rapport with the candidate before you meet and gain some first impressions (although don't be too reliant on these).

6. Never run a group interview session without first setting out clear ground rules and criteria for judgement. You will waste a lot of time arguing over trivialities if you don't have a clear framework.

7. The appraisal interview needs more care and preparation time. Make sure you know what you want to achieve but coax the interviewee into reaching his or her

own conclusions about weaknesses and make realistic
goals which can be mutually agreed.

8. Develop a tight structure and consistent procedure for
all disciplinary interviews. Make sure you get the facts
straight, keep detailed notes and be aware of the
statutory rights of the interviewee.

What's in this chapter for you

> *Why you should prepare*
> *Finding out about the interviewee*
> *Telling the candidate about the job*
> *Telling the candidate about the your organisation*
> *Telling the candidate about the interview*
> *Preparing the support staff*
> *Preparing the interviewer/s*

> **"** *To be honest, I never have much time to prepare to give an interview. I like it that way: I get a buzz from going into an interview room knowing nothing about the candidate or even the details of the job on offer.* **"**
> **– Bill Samuel, sales director**

Why you should prepare

Bill is kidding himself. It's a great excuse to be lazy – "It's better not to prepare". Whilst you never want an interview to be too scripted and formulaic, there are definite advantages in being well prepared.

Poorly prepared interviews are to be avoided. They are:

○ *unfair on the candidates*
○ *likely to be inconsistent between candidates*
○ *wasteful of time and resources*
○ *unlikely to select the best choice.*

Poor planning also indicates to the candidate that, in this respect at least, the company is badly organised and cavalier in its attitude to new recruits. A sure sign of a badly planned interview is that the interviewer ends up doing too much talking.

What would you feel if somebody interviewing you obviously knew nothing about you while you had spent a lot of valuable time finding out about the organisation?

There is another pressing reason to prepare for an interview. A mistake can cost an organisation a lot of money. Think of the time and cost of recruiting, training, inducting, and supervising someone who turns out to be not up to the job. Add to this the costs in staff time of an inefficient, possibly badly motivated and even disruptive person on the team. Yes, getting the interview wrong can be very expensive.

Preparation time is time well spent. In the end it can save a lot of money. Think of it as a good investment.

When you interview people, how much time do you give to preparation? Is it enough?

A well-planned interview aims at allowing both sides to glean the information they need to make an informed judgement. Remember: it is a two-way process. The interviewee has come to find out more about you and your organisation.

Finding out about the interviewee

An essential part of the interview preparation is finding out as much as possible about the interviewees before you meet them.

> ❝ *We send out a pretty detailed application form and ask for a CV. I make sure that we read these forms thoroughly before meeting the candidate.* ❞
> – **June Flinn, director of a food processing company**

Why, do you think, is it important to find out as much as possible about the candidate before meeting them?

An interview is a short snapshot out of a person's life. In an hour (more or less) you may have to make a judgement that could have a massive effect on the person and the organisation. Your decision may involve a complete shift in the person's life: where they live, how they spend their leisure time, their future career.

The stakes are high – the highest: we are talking about people's lives and livelihoods.

The background facts about a candidate are necessary because these are the things you should know before talking to them. They will form the basis of what you may want to ask them. They will begin the process of informing you about the candidates: their background, abilities and experience.

Take a look at the application forms and CV requirements your organisation currently asks for. Do they elicit enough detail about the interviewee? The key test is whether you waste too much time in interviews asking questions like:

❑ *Where have you worked before?*
❑ *How long were you at your last job?*
❑ *What are your qualifications?*
❑ *What is your current salary?*
❑ *Where do you now live?*

All of the above and other purely factual questions should be answered before the interview takes place. You really shouldn't be wasting valuable interview time asking such questions. (Besides, it looks amateurish and inane to ask such fundamental questions as "Now Miss Brown, how old are you? Where did you go to school?")

Use an application form or the CV to get information on candidates such as:

○ **Personal:** age, marital status, address, education, training, qualifications and interests.
○ **Employment history:** current position and responsibilities, current salary, previous jobs and achievements etc.

Telling the candidate about the job

❝ *We make sure that before the interviewee comes, we tell them about the job they will be doing, should they be successful. It's essential to get this right. Make it clear what responsibilities are to be expected. You should never leave this information until*

the interview. Send it out as a written description or discuss it over the telephone. **"**
– June Flinn

June is right. Candidates for a job need and expect to be told in detail what the job will ask of them. If you fail to do this, blame yourself for getting the wrong people to interview.

Does any of this sound like you? If so, it's time to change your methods.

- ❑ *"Advertising space is very expensive, I usually leave the details of the job until the candidate comes to interview."*
- ❑ *"We never like to mention salary or working conditions until the interview stage, that way we don't get people coming for the wrong reasons."*
- ❑ *"I prefer to describe the job face-to-face rather than put it in print."*

Withholding details is very unfair to the candidates. It is also very inefficient. If advertising is too expensive, at least put the job details down on an information sheet, or discuss them over the phone. It is also pointless and irritating to leave out details such as salaries, fringe benefits and conditions of employment. Interviewees will probably think you've got something to hide.

Here is a useful checklist of things you should tell candidates well before they come for interview. How you tell them is up to you – in writing, as part of the application form pack, by telephone. . .

- ❑ *What the job asks of them – what their duties and tasks will be, and the level of skill and ability expected.*
- ❑ *The level and amount of experience you expect from a successful applicant.*
- ❑ *What the terms and conditions of service are (including salary, holidays, benefits, hours etc.).*
- ❑ *When the job is to begin and how long it will last if it's a temporary position.*

❝ *We try to tell the candidate as much about the job as possible. We don't believe in hiding anything and, even if there are minus points, we don't avoid telling them. Last week, I sent out an application pack including a four-page form, guidelines for the CV, a two-sided job description and comments from existing employees. We also had a "downside" list – things to expect that may not always be so welcome – like "expect to do a lot of overtime in the summer" or "the pressure at the end of the season can be intense" or, even, "some say the boss can be very intimidating". The more truthful and honest you are, the more likely you are to get the right person coming with realistic expectations. But don't forget to say nice things too.* ❞

– June Flinn

It's not very usual, but think about including the opinions of current staff in your job description.

Telling the candidate about your organisation

Remember that an interview is a two-way process. It's not just about assessing a candidate: it is also your duty to tell the interviewee about you and your organisation. Job selection also means job acceptance.

❝ *We usually include quite a bit of information about our company in the application pack. This is for three reasons: it's only fair that a prospective employee should know about us so that he or she can make an informed decision on whether to accept a job offer. Secondly, we hope that it may stimulate the interviewee into asking relevant questions about us. Lastly, the more they know about our company, the more they can relate the job description to the overall strategy of our business. They get a picture of where they would fit into the overall scheme of things.* ❞

– Bob Pector, manager in a paint spray firm

How much information does your organisation give to prospective employees about itself? Is it enough to tell the candidates all they are likely to want to know before you interview them?

How much should you tell them? There are some obvious things to include and exclude. You wouldn't, for instance, want to give away sensitive information or anything that can be used to advantage by a competitor.

> **"** *A few years ago we ran a rather daft job advertisement that said we had plans to expand into the Midlands area and were looking for a suitable area manager. This gave our competitors in the Birmingham region plenty of time to plan their campaign against us. We're still struggling to get business there.* **"**
> **– Lucy Gresham, MD of a parts distributor**

So, what do you tell them? Here are some essentials:

○ *Your company history – maybe not too much detail but show them how you got to where you are today.*

○ *Company structure and organisation – show them where they would fit into the business. How does the department they would work for link into the whole organisation? What are the levels of responsibility? Who would they report to?*

○ *Product or service profile – what does the organisation produce? Some companies send a full technical product specifications, others a brief outline.*

○ *Organisational culture – what is the mission statement, what are its beliefs and standards? Typical ones are: "To achieve maximum customer satisfaction" or "To grow to be a major player in our market".*

○ *Staff relations – the kind of organisation atmosphere: friendly, informal, are free thinkers encouraged? Will the interviewee have to fit into a more rigid structure?*

○ *Future directions – where is the organisation heading? How can a new recruit help it towards its goals? This information may be sensitive so think carefully about what you will say.*

> **"** *Once I had the feeling that an interviewee was from a rival company trying to sniff out our future plans. You have to be careful.* **"**
> **– Lucy Gresham**

Some organisations like to send their annual report, staff newsletters, company brochures. This is a good idea. The more the candidate knows about your organisation *before* the interview, the more successful it should be.

As well as these useful background points about an

organisation's culture and structure, you should also send practical information about the company. This might include details of the career structure (if any) – candidates will want to know what prospects there are for their career development. Be honest and realistic. Avoid: "The sky's the limit with this job" or "Expect to be a Board member within two years". Unrealistic promises only serve to raise unfulfillable expectations – not good for staff morale. People may feel cheated if once in post they realise that what was told to them at interview was untrue.

Also describe any fringe benefits that might be enjoyed – such as staff discounts, travel perks, car parking allowance and so on.

Look again at what information your organisation sends out to prospective interviewees. Is it enough and of the right quality? Suggest ways how it can be improved to colleagues.

Telling the candidate about the interview

 " *I find that interviews go better if we remember to inform the candidate about the process – what he or she can expect on the day. Who will be talking to them. What will we be looking for. How long will it all take.* "
– Mark Fisher, MD of fax paper company

Mark is right. The key to successful interviewing is to minimise the unexpected. Just as you should know as much as possible about the candidates, so they should know what will happen to them on interview day. The more they know, the less likely they will be unnecessarily stressed (there is no greater fear than that of the unknown). It is in your interests to have interviewees who are in control of the situation, and feel calm and collected enough to give a true picture of themselves.

 " *When we invite people to interview, we always send them a full letter and maps giving details of the day, who they will meet, times and locations. We also try, although it's not always possible, to say what will happen during the interview.* "
– Mark Fisher

Think back to your last interview (as a candidate). How much did you know about the day? Did you feel that you should have been told more?

> **"** *The last interview I went to, the company deliberately kept the candidates in the dark. No proper details of the job description, terms and conditions were given. Their strategy was to tell us individually as we went in for the interview. As it turned out, it was a job I would not have accepted. I wondered why the company was so secretive. The result was the most candidates on the day were suspicious and demotivated. It gave a very poor impression of the company.* **"**
> **– Mark Lee, marketing manager**

Mark's experience is all too common. Many companies like to keep their interviewees in the dark (for reasons that are not at all clear). This is very bad practice (unless there are overriding security issues at stake) and should be avoided. Tell more, tell all.

Here are some of the things you could tell interviewees about their day with you:

- ○ *Where they need to go* – it's a good idea to send a map and travel instructions, including bus, train or taxi information where necessary. If parking is a problem, say so, and give advice about where they can go. Show this on your map. Many companies now have ready-made travel instructions and map. Don't forget to give instructions from all directions.
- ○ *When they need to arrive* – give the time and the day. It's a good idea to ask them to report in say 10–15 minutes before the interview begins. That way they can find their way and get settled.
- ○ *To whom they should report* – if you want them to go to reception, say so and make sure they know where this is. Reception areas in many small companies are often difficult to find and hidden behind unmarked doors.
- ○ *Who they will meet at the interview* – this is especially important where there is a panel of interviewers. Give details of the interviewer's role and responsibility. Here is an example:
  "Your interview will begin at 10.30 a.m. in the Edinburgh Building. It will be conducted by Brian Moore, head of corporate planning, Jill Young, assistant marketing controller and Fran Smethurst, production manager . . ."

○ How the interview will be structured – if there is an interview plan (and there should be – see chapter five), they should be given details. You could tell them: what they will be questioned about, what exercises, role plays, simulations or presentations they will be asked to give, and more details about the role of each interviewer in the process. As an example:

"Ms Young will discuss the marketing aspects of the post and will explore your marketing background, ideas you may have for furthering the customer base of the organisation and how you would fit into our existing team . . ."

○ When the interview is likely to end – this is important for the interviewees' travel arrangements.

○ What further interviews, assessments or other selection events will take place should they be successful at the first round.

○ What they must bring with them – this might include portfolios, samples of work, testimonials and so on.

○ What they should do if they cannot attend the arranged interview.

Look at the information currently sent out to interviewees. Ask colleagues to think about how it can be extended and improved so that interviewees are better informed.

Preparing the support staff

Unless you are interviewing someone for a one-person business, it is likely that a candidate will come across other people during the course of the interview day. The way these support staff are managed can have a profound effect on the impression the interviewee gains. They can do a lot of good in reinforcing positive messages about the organisation; they can also do untold harm to your image and the messages of the interview.

        ❝ The last interview I went to was going really well. They seemed to like me and I was impressed by the image they gave me of the company. It seemed to be an informal place where everyone's views were respected and new ideas encouraged. That's what they told me. But over lunch, which I had by myself, I met one of the older supervisors. He asked if I'd come for the job and then told me what a terrible company it was. He went on: "I'm glad to be getting out soon. They never listen to what you say. And the boss? She may seem all sweetness and light today, but you wait till your

till your working for her. Terrible temper." His mates all agreed. I
was so put off that I refused the job. 99
– Sam Green, unemployed graduate

If an interviewee comes to your organisation, think of the different people he or she is likely to meet that day – from car park attendant, lift operator, receptionist, canteen worker, PA, other employees and managers, maybe even customers.

Although it's not always easy, you should do your best to prepare support and other staff for the visit by interviewees. This could be done as a memo or part of a training exercise. Make sure that:

○ *Reception staff know that the interviewees are coming and are ready to welcome and assist them. See that coffees, teas or other refreshments are offered and any facilities explained.*
○ *PAs know where to take the interviewees and what the pattern of the day will be. Where will the candidates wait? What about lunch and toilet facilities? What happens after the interview – do they go or stay? Are they given travel expenses on the spot? What about follow-up information?*
○ *Other staff are warned to expect to see interviewees. Emphasise the need to be courteous and positive but not to discuss the job on offer. If there is to be a tour of the site, inform supervisors in advance so that they can be ready for the visit.*

66 *Before another interview I had we did a tour of the factory. Everyone looked really happy and pleased to see us – it gave us all a very good impression of the company.* 99
– Sam Green

What policy do you have for support and other employees during an interview session? Review what you do, how you do it and any improvements that need to be discussed.

Preparing the interviewers

This may include yourself and/or a team of interview panellists. How do you prepare? Here are two contrasting views:

❝ *We spend as long preparing for an interview as we do actually interviewing. We realise that it takes a lot of time but we are talking about a major investment here – people are our lifeblood.* ❞
– Bill Perry, engineer

❝ *We have so little time that there isn't much preparation. We have a standard crib sheet with model questions and a few aims and objectives, and then we all play it by ear.* ❞
– Damon Firth, telesales manager

The key message of this book is that a successful interview only comes from careful planning. It should not be left to pure chance. If you are leading a team of interviewers you should discuss with them:

○ *who they will be seeing*
○ *the candidates' backgrounds (from the CVs and application forms)*
○ *what the interview structure will be – the role of each interviewer, what they are trying to find out about the person, what will happen during the interview and beyond*

❝ *We always have a briefing session with interviewers – actually we have two: one a day or so before the event so that we can talk about arrangements and structure, and one on the day to talk about the candidates and what we will be trying to find out about them.* ❞
– Bill Perry

What do interviewers need to know? Any briefing session with the team should include the following points.

(1) About the vacancy

The job – what is it? How does it fit into the corporate strategy? How long will it last? What objectives are being set? How will it be measured?

The skills needed – what are you looking for in terms of skills, ability, knowledge, experience? The more objective you can be the better. The job specification should be as detailed as possible so that you know who the ideal candidate would be. Each aspect of the job should be covered. As an example:

❝ *We need someone with IT skills – word processing, typing up to grade xxx, ability to use database software – good telephone skills, experience in running an office, and proven sales ability. . .* ❞

It might be a good idea to mark these requirements on a table or checklist so that you can judge each candidate against these criteria.

(2) Prospects offered

What prospects are there in this particular position for training, for career development, salary and benefits, growth etc. that you can use to tempt candidates?

(3) Objectives

What must be elicited from the interviewees – their background, their knowledge, their personality, their ability to fit into the existing team and so on?

❝ *If we use a team of interviewers, we work out in advance who is going to ask which questions. It saves a lot of confusion!* ❞
– Bill Perry

Each person on the team must understand his or her role and function. Why are they there? What speciality are they expected to bring to the session? What should they be looking for in an interviewee?

(4) Understanding the limits

Interviewers should be aware of their rights to offer anything to candidates. This is most important. The team must be briefed on what can and cannot be offered.

❝ *When one of the panel asked me, "What would you say to being moved to our USA office?" I was surprised when the senior interviewer interrupted and said, "That won't be possible I'm afraid." It didn't look good to me.* ❞
– Keith Phillips, IT director

Make sure that you or your colleagues are empowered to make offers, claims, negotiate reward packages, location, starting dates and so on.

(5) Don't break the law

Terms of employment are covered by laws, agreements and court rulings. Make sure you all fully understand the law as it relates to:

- *equal rights*
- *discrimination on the grounds of race, gender, religion or disability*
- *unfair dismissal*
- *disciplinary procedures.*

In the UK failure to comply with employment and anti-discrimination laws can lead to the criminal or civil action in courts or industrial tribunals. Take great care over what is said, done and offered at a job interview.

Look again at how your organisation briefs its interviewers. Is there anything you could learn from the points above? Identify any weaknesses and suggest improvements to your current practice.

The art of preparation in a nutshell

1. Commit to spending as much time in preparation as in interviewing – it's money well spent.
2. Send as much information as possible to the interviewees before the interview – and don't forget their needs. Interviewees should be given all the information they need to make their way to the interview without trouble, they should know precisely what the job involves and what to expect from the session.
3. Check over your current application forms and CV guidelines (if any). Will they supply you with all the details about the candidate you want? If not, change them.
4. Send the candidates lots of information about your organisation – make sure it is relevant and does not reveal anything sensitive.

5. Be clear and honest about your terms and conditions of employment, including salary and benefits, and details of any down-sides of the position (e.g. unavoidable overtime at busy times). There may be minimum requirements set by legislation or by agreements with trades unions, staff associations or national employer bodies.

6. Brief all your support staff and anyone who will come into contact with the interviewees. Make sure any messages they give are consistent with company policy.

7. Brief your interviewers – make sure they know all about the job on offer and which qualities, skills, abilities, experience and knowledge are required. Ensure also that each of them knows his or her role and the limits of what they can offer.

8. Sharpen up your own abilities to read and assess the candidates – read on for more.

What's in this chapter for you

> *How to listen*
> *How to empathise*
> *How to read body language*
> *How to put people at ease*

❝ *Interviewing is both an art and a science. It's something people can be naturally good at – but, at the same time, everyone can improve. It's all a matter of honing the basic skills.* ❞
— **Steve Butler, HR director**

This chapter looks at some of the key skills you need to be an ace interviewer, and how to get them.

How to listen

Listening is a rare skill. Few people are good at it and, as we get older, it seems that we get worse. And it's nothing to do with our physical ability to hear.

> Is this you? "Yes, of course, I'm a good listener – everyone is!" Actually, most people aren't, so think again.

Listening has everything to do with how we use our ears to take in the messages we are getting. It's an ability not just to hear but to listen to:

○ *What is being said – the words used*
○ *How it is being said – the tone of voice*
○ *What is NOT being said – what the speaker is communicating unintentionally through his or her nervousness or is holding back.*

Listening is an **active** skill. It's hard work and needs our full attention – ears, eyes and brain.

> How do your rate your listening skills? Do you:
>
> ❑ *Switch off from people when you don't agree with them?*
> ❑ *Always think you know what the other person is going to say?*

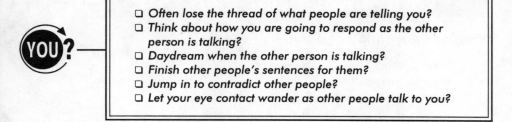

- ❏ *Often lose the thread of what people are telling you?*
- ❏ *Think about how you are going to respond as the other person is talking?*
- ❏ *Daydream when the other person is talking?*
- ❏ *Finish other people's sentences for them?*
- ❏ *Jump in to contradict other people?*
- ❏ *Let your eye contact wander as other people talk to you?*

These are all signs of poor listening skills. And most of us are guilty of some of them. How often do we see people losing interest in a conversation unless it is about them, or waiting impatiently for their turn to have a say?

It might be a good idea to ask others what they think of you. A good interviewer is above all an excellent listener. The problem with poor listening is that it means poorer communication. And communication is the key to good interviewing. It is a two-way thing. It is an analytical process of taking in what is being said – the levels of meaning, the tone and nuances.

> ❝ *I could tell the interviewer wasn't listening. The temptation to chip in a sentence about my kleptomania was almost irresistible!* ❞
> **– anonymous job hunter**

Poor listening comes from years of filtering out all the stuff we didn't want to know or hear. We develop strategies for poor listening – nodding in agreement, butting in, finishing people's sentences for them etc. The trick is to overcome these bad habits.

Tips on good listening

- ❏ *Practice keeping eye contact with people speaking to you. Don't let your gaze wander or spend the whole interview looking at your notes and muttering "ah ha" or "I see yes...". Eye contact is the key to expressing your interest. If the candidate is boring you, try to steer the conversation on to something more stimulating.*
- ❏ *Listen out for the real message that is being given. What is the person trying to tell you. Get behind the words and understand what the candidate is trying to communicate.*
- ❏ *Don't cut people off or interrupt. Start listening to yourself. Watch and listen to what you do when other people are talking.*

- ❏ *Stop yourself trying to judge the other person's character all the time. Just listen, and consider what you have discovered about them later.*
- ❏ *Don't pretend to listen. The other person probably knows when you have "switched off". This can be extremely irritating and seen as a slight. You are in danger of alienating your interviewee.*
- ❏ *Formulate what you are going to say only after the other person has finished. If you are in the habit of doing so while the other person is still talking to you, you aren't listening!*

Another common bad habit is trying to second guess what the other person is going to say. Here is a typical (bad) example:

- ○ *Interviewer: Tell me why you left your last job.*
- ○ *Candidate: Well I'd been in the post for five years and . . .*
- ○ *Interviewer: I know, you got bored . . .*
- ○ *Candidate: No, it wasn't that. I had been product manager . . .*
- ○ *Interviewer: . . . And you felt stuck in the post? You wanted to get out, yes?*
- ○ *Candidate: No, I enjoyed being product manager . . .*
- ○ *Interviewer: . . . But you felt undervalued and maybe frustrated?*
- ○ *Candidate: Not really . . .*

You can see how this discussion is going nowhere fast. If the interviewer stopped guessing what the candidate thought and just listened he would find out what really happened.

How to empathise

> **❝** *What makes a good interviewer? I would say, above all, the ability to empathise with your candidate.* **❞**
> **– Alf Marshall, CEO of hi-tech supplies business**

Do you understand what is meant by "empathy"? This is one of the most widely misunderstood terms. It is not to be confused with "sympathy". It is not feeling sorry for the other person, nor is it wanting the other side to do well. It's nothing to do with any moral judgements we may make; it doesn't even mean we have to agree with the other person.

Empathy is mutual understanding, an insight into what the other person is saying and why they are saying it. Empathy can lead to increased mutual goodwill – but not always. I may know exactly why you are taking a certain stand, why you are saying certain things but disagree with them profoundly. Empathy comes from good listening and keen observation of others. It is all about establishing rapport and "getting into the mind" of the other person.

Here are some simple techniques to help you empathise with interviewees

- ❑ *Break the ice. Try to find out what the other person is really interested in and get them to tell you about it. For example, you could say: "I see from your CV that you are interested in Elizabethan aircraft. Tell me more. What is it that fascinates you?" There is nothing like getting people to talk about their own pet interests and activities.*
- ❑ *Find areas of mutual interest. Empathy is all about confidence building and establishing that both sides can communicate. It's easier to empathise with someone who has similar tastes and interests.*
- ❑ *If you can't find areas of mutual interest, get the candidate to talk about something they feel really confident about. The most common subject is their journey to the interview (or the weather). At least they are on sure ground here and you can demonstrate that you are genuinely interested in what they say rather than going through the motions.*
- ❑ *Use all the positive techniques of communication such as keen listening and reinforcing body language to "get into the skin" of the other person. What are they trying to tell you?*

How to read body language

There is a lot of nonsense talked about body language – as though it is some kind of complex alternative means of communication. In face, body language simply involves using your eyes to observe the non-verbal communication we are all capable of. As all humans use their bodies to communicate (as well as sounds), it is a language we all know. We don't have to be taught that a person's body is telling us that they are tense, nervous or confident, smug or bluffing. We use this body talk all the time, the trick is to use your eyes to see it. Body language recognition is just like good listening skills – it is a question of being tuned in to what the other person is saying, thinking and feeling.

Constantly monitor yourself to make sure you don't display the tell-tale body language signs that say, "I am bored with your talk and I'm not really listening". These include yawning, looking at the ceiling, checking your watch, foot tapping, eyes fixed elsewhere or on others.

You can read a person's body language just by watching them carefully (without, of course, rudely staring). Here are some classics. You can probably read what they mean already.

- ○ *Knees locked together, arms tightly folded, hunched posture, sweating – signs of probable tension.*
- ○ *Fixed smile or stony face, watch checking, eyebrow raising, humming, tapping pen on teeth, chewing pencil, chewing nails, fidgeting, ear pulling, head scratching, leaning back with hands behind the head, swivelling in the chair, shuffling papers, foot tapping – signs of probable boredom in what is being said.*
- ○ *Folding arms, looking away pointedly, shaking head, throat clearing, sitting forward aggressively with legs apart, pointing a finger, clenching and banging fists – signs of irritation or anger.*

Your interviewee may display these and other body language signs. Interpretation is easy, observation is the difficult bit. Just be aware of how the other person is sitting, what they are doing with their hands, what mannerisms they are displaying. Remember also that reading body language is a two-way process. The interviewee will be watching yours.

Here are some positive and reassuring types of body language

- ❑ *Always face the other person and maintain sharp eye contact at all times – but don't stare. Look interested and lively.*
- ❑ *Lean towards the speaker rather than away from them.*
- ❑ *Nod in agreement to show that you are following their conversation. Make responsive noises and sound as though you mean them!*
- ❑ *Smile – it will make you both feel better. Remember that if you feel happy to smile it will also show in your eyes.*

> ❑ *Assume and maintain a relaxed open posture. Keep your hands still or gesticulate while you talk. Don't fidget, chew nails or juggle with paper clips.*

You cannot really fake body language. To do all the right things as above, you need to feel right about the interviewee. You need to want to make them feel comfortable and at ease.

> Think about any bad body language habits you have got into. Watch yourself on video or ask a friend to comment on your mannerisms – especially those you tend to use once other people are speaking. Also, next time you are in discussion with someone, or are conducting an interview, watch out for their body language. Start to observe people more closely.

How to put people at ease

Part of your job as an interviewer is to put the candidates at ease. If the interviewee feels comfortable you will find it far easier to get whatever information you want from them.

> How do you feel about this opinion? "I like an interview to have a certain amount of tension in it. It's not good to be too cosy."

There is actually no point in making an interviewee unnecessarily tense or uneasy. You want to see them as they would be in the workplace, not under unusually stressful conditions. Some people completely dry up when nervous, can't think clearly, can't speak properly, can't say what they mean. As interviewing is all about communication, your job as director of the session, is to ensure a calm, relaxed (OK, not too relaxed) atmosphere. How do you achieve it? Here are some quick methods you can use.

> How to establish the right atmosphere
>
> ❑ *Allow plenty of time for both interviewers and interviewees to settle in before starting. Offer interviewees coffee and get*

someone to chat to them while they wait. Don't leave interviewees on their own for too long.

❏ Have a 20-minute briefing session for the interviewers to get their thoughts straight, and their strategy clearly worked out.

❏ Make the interview room as comfortable as possible. Make sure it is clean and tidy, warm enough, with water or other soft drinks available and easily accessible. Where possible and appropriate, arrange the room in an informal manner. There is nothing more forbidding than an interviewer sitting behind a huge desk at the far end of the room.

❏ Collect the interviewee yourself and show him or her to the seat, with a friendly gesture. Use small talk to break the ice – try to be relaxed and friendly.

Whether as interviewer or interviewee, try to relax yourself before the session. Take in some nice, slow, deep breaths. Close your eyes and concentrate only on your breathing for at least two minutes. Concentrate only on the rhythmical breathing you can hear. Slow the breathing down and try to push out your diaphragm as you breath out.

Breathing really can be used to improve your ability to relax. Invest in some good relaxation tapes and learn the art of good breathing.

Here is an example of how not to conduct an interview.

❝ My worst interview was with a university examining board. As a candidate for a job I was left to wait outside a room. Then I had to knock on the door to find beyond a huge, forbidding oak-panelled room with eight people sitting behind a large raised desk. Each interviewer was wearing a college robe. I had no idea it was going to be that formal – I didn't even know it was going to be a panel interview. Needless to say, I was completely lost for words. ❞
– Bev Collar, exams officer

Think about interviews you have attended. What was done to make you relaxed and comfortable? What should have been done to improve the atmosphere?

How to improve your interviewing skills

1. Start by analysing honestly your own listening skills. What are you good at? What could be improved?
2. Video yourself or get someone to talk to you and give feedback about what you do when you are listening to others, especially in an interview. The more you know about yourself as a listener, the more self-aware you will be – so much the better.
3. Practice picking up on what people are really saying – this means listening very carefully and trying to understand what is actually being said. People often lose the thread of what they are trying to communicate.
4. Avoid interrupting others or trying to finish their sentences for them.
5. Never pretend to listen. You will be found out and alienate the interviewee.

6. Learn how to empathise by looking for topics of mutual interest – this will help to break the ice with interviewees.
7. Pay attention to body language. Use your eyes and your brain to work out what people are telling you from the way they sit, stand or move. Look at the ways of giving positive body language signals and practice using them. Remember, it's a two-way process.
8. Always maintain eye contact and an interested gaze – this will encourage candidates into giving more.
9. Never stoop to being pompous in situations where your are interviewing people who are so far below you on the ladder you need binoculars to see them. Humility always helps.
10. Learn the simple techniques of relaxing yourself – if you are a relaxed interviewer, your interviewees will feel far more comfortable and open.

What's in this chapter for you

Things to check before the interview starts
How to start an interview
The "meat" of the interview
Assessing the evidence
Ways to deal with difficult interviewees
Concluding the interview

> ❝ By the time I go into the interview, I know as much as I possibly can about the candidate, and I've verified that the candidate has been given full information about the organisation, the vacant post and the structure of the interview. From careful planning I also know precisely what the objectives of the interview are – what skills, experience, knowledge and ability I'm looking for. ❞
> **– Lucy McLucre, Headhunter**

Do you know what attributes the perfect applicant will have before you go into an interview, and how to find out if the person in front of you has them? You should, and this is why thorough preparation is essential.

Although it's unlikely you will ever recruit Superman or Superwoman, you need to know what your ideal candidate will be like. Use this as a basis on which to judge the lesser mortals you are bound to see.

Never again go into an interview unprepared. Make this an unbreakable resolution – there is too much at stake. Remember: "A professional interview is 90 per cent in the preparation."

Things to check before the interview starts

Here are some useful guidelines from experienced interviewers. Treat this as a checklist.

○ *Does the candidate know where to come and when to arrive?*

○ *Does the candidate know what information, portfolio examples, assessment forms and so on, to bring?*

○ *Have the other interviewers and the support staff been informed and briefed?*

○ *Do you know enough about the job or issue under discussion? Can you recall the key facts without resorting to notes during the interview?*

○ *Are you relaxed, calm and ready to exude an air of friendly confidence?*

○ *Has the interview room been properly organised? Does it suit the purpose – i.e. does the room layout fit the type of interview?*

○ *Don't forget the waiting room – make it bright and comfortable with things there for candidates to read (maybe the company brochure or newsletter). Initial impressions are important in setting the tone.*

On the subject of the interview room, there are several ways to lay it out. If you intend to conduct a very formal interview, then the traditional layout is the "star chamber". The lone interviewee sits before the panel of interviewers. For more informal sessions, chairs can be arranged in a circle or semicircle (this encourages free discussion). You may even decide to hold the interview in a very laid-back area such as the coffee room. But beware of the subliminal messages you may be sending – low status room = low status post.

Whatever your layout, try to avoid the interviewee being distanced from the panel.

> **"** *At my last interview, I had to get up each time I wanted to take a biscuit or fill my coffee cup. The interviewers seemed to be about ten feet away. It made the whole thing very intimidating and impersonal.* **"**
> **another anonymous job hunter**

How to start an interview

Kicking off an interview is often the hardest thing. It can make or break the effectiveness of the process. So, how do you get the ball rolling when everyone, including the interviewers, feels nervous?

> Remember that your key aim in the opening minutes is to create an atmosphere where the candidate can open up and feel confident about speaking.

A recommended starting point is to bring the candidate into the interview room yourself. This allows you to begin with pleasantries and small talk – start to build a rapport.

> Here are some more useful tips from veterans of the interview room.
>
> ❑ *If there is anyone else in the room, get them to introduce themselves and explain their role and position. This will reinforce what you have told the interviewee about the structure of the interview.*
> ❑ *Begin with an introduction and outline the purpose of the interview so the interviewee has time to settle.*
> ❑ *Establish early on whether and when the candidate can and should ask questions. For most interviews, this will be important. An interview should be a two-way affair.*

The "meat" of the interview

Once the introductions are over, and everyone is settled, you now get down to the main part of the interview. A well-planned session should follow a pre-planned, systematic approach. The plan will differ for each interview, but it should contain a set of questions that you will ask each of the candidates. These questions are aimed at eliciting all of the information you want from the candidates:

○ *finding out what level of expertise they possess*
○ *running down the qualities needed in the job description to see how closely the candidate fits them*
○ *establishing how honest and reliable is the information they have given in the CV or application form*
○ *testing the candidates' vision of how they will move the organisation or department forward, or how they see themselves in the post*

○ *testing their knowledge of the subject – checking to see if it is up to the standard the job requires*
○ *observing the candidates' behaviour – trying to assess their personality and whether they will fit into the current team*
○ *assessing each candidate's ability to fulfil the tactical and strategic targets set by the organisation.*

If the position is managerial, you will need also to assess the candidate's ability to handle people, plan, monitor, set budgets, deal with problems and crises, handle stress and other perceived qualities that the "ideal" candidate should possess.

Observing the candidate

We have largely dealt with this in the last chapter. But remember that a skilled interviewer will analyse what the person says, how it is said and what body language messages are being given. Observation means using all your senses to assess the situation. Do the candidate's words match his or her body language? If not, you may need to use more probing questioning. Check the evidence without being accusatory. Let the candidate do most of the talking.

> Next time you conduct an interview, ask yourself whether you are using all of your observational skills. It is not enough to read from a list of prepared questions. Remember to watch, listen and understand.

Assessing the evidence

The interviewee is there to provide evidence of his or her ability to do the job (or answer a disciplinary charge, provide an assessment of their work and so on). This evidence should never be taken at face value. It needs to be checked and double-checked. Assessing evidence is a skill in its own right. You need to be part counsellor, part detective. Few candidates will lie about the facts (well, a few might). What we all do is exaggerate the truth to put our qualities in the best light. We've all tried to hide mistakes or cover up errors of judgement. Here are a couple of useful ideas about how to improve your ability to assess the evidence.

Check each claim made in the application form or CV

Where possible ask a subject expert to delve deeper. Get the candidate to talk about his or her stated strengths. Here is an example:

Candidate claims that she has wide experience of PC and Mac software, and has dealt extensively with customer service matters. Interviewer asks her the following questions:

"I see that you have worked with both PCs and Macs. Could you tell us about that. Which system do you think would work best in our environment?"

"Can you give us some examples of how you have helped your current organisation achieve a higher level of customer care?"

Use a rating system

Grading the interviewees is easier if you devise a simple rating system that compares the candidate's performance to a set of job-related criteria. Here is an example.

What we want: rating 1 (= unacceptable) to 10 (= excellent)

- ❑ *Knowledge of the job*
- ❑ *Experience in running a department*
- ❑ *A foreign language at negotiation level*
- ❑ *Ability to handle crises*
- ❑ *Ability to run a large budget*
- ❑ *Experience in dealing with staff motivation*
- ❑ *Assembling skills*
- ❑ *IT skills*

As you can see, some of these qualities can be tested easily. It is sometimes more difficult to assess how the candidate would react or act in a hypothetical situation, one they haven't yet faced. You may of course ask them what they would do, or get them to complete a role-play exercise. You can also explore how well they have faced up to new challenges in the past. Remember, that you are looking for their ability to become an excellent employee. It is their potential you are testing, not just their past history.

> 66 *After hearing the experiences he talked of in the interview, I was confused by the lack of career progression reflected in John's CV so I followed up by contacting the referees he'd put forward. I now know he'd suffered at the hands of an autocratic manager in a stifling organisational culture but felt it would be unprofessional to mention it explicitly in the interview. I'm glad to say he's now one of our best team leaders.* 99
> **– Mark Fisher, paper merchant MD**

Wherever possible try to use two or more pieces of evidence to corroborate your impressions of interviewees. Don't guess – look for hard evidence. Ask yourself how the ratings given match the other evidence you have. Why, for instance, might the evidence on paper suggest a rather poor people manager, when the person sitting in front of you seems very confident and gives the impression of being very competent in this area. Check the written evidence. Ask other questions which test the candidate's managerial abilities.

> 66 *I sometimes like to act as devil's advocate. I may think a person is just right for the job but ask my colleagues on the panel to tell me why I'm wrong. This way I'm likely to get a more balanced view.* 99
> **– Guy Webster, personnel manager in optics**

Dealing with difficult interviewees

People come in all shapes and sizes, and with even more varied personalities. Not every interviewee is the modest, rational and truthful soul you can rely on to tell you all you need to know. In today's tight job markets, you may be dealing with candidates who can pick and choose between jobs. Here are some typical tougher customers and how to deal with them.

The silent lamb

This kind won't say anything – except maybe the odd murmur or affirmation. Not everyone is good at talking – especially about themselves in tense circumstances. It may not be so important for the postholder to be verbally communicative but you still need to find out more about them. What do you do?

○ *Work harder at establishing a rapport. Try your best to find common ground – something, anything, they are interested in. The trick is to get them to open up.*
○ *Make the interview less formal. Call a halt to a session that isn't going anywhere. Take a break to get more coffee (and thumbscrews). Rearrange chairs and tables, cut the panel size down, whatever – make the session more conducive to chatting.*
○ *If the person prefers to put things in writing, let them do it. Give them time to answer.*

Never try to bully or cajole the person into talking. It will do more harm than good.

Chatterbox

We have all met them – interviewees who relish the thought of talking about themselves without interruption. It is often the sign of self-doubt. Occasionally it may be a huge ego at work. More often than not, it is a sign of nerves. The candidate has thought so long and hard about this interview that once they start, they cannot stop. What do you do?

○ *Try to calm the candidate with some small-talk.*
○ *Be assertive. Wait for a suitable pause and say: "Well that seems to have answered my question very fully, let's go on to the next."*
○ *Ask lots of closed questions (those that can be answered with a simple yes or no).*
○ *Set a time limit on answers. Tell them that they have about three minutes per answer and they should think for a moment or two before speaking.*
○ *Remind the candidate how much time there is left to go. Be polite in doing so.*
○ *Remind them that they will have time to ask questions or air their views later in the interview.*

Cool customer

Some interviewees like to show that they are unfazed by the experience, that they really don't need the job and that they are doing you a favour by being there. They may be playing hard to get hoping to raise the rewards of getting the job. They may be naturally assertive types who like to be in control. What do you do?

○ *Maintain the initiative. Do not let the interviewee set the agenda*
○ *Be assertive: ask your questions with quiet confidence and determination.*

○ *Avoid being rude or aggressive – if you don't, you will just fall into their trap.*

○ *Emphasise that they will have their chance to ask questions **later**.*

○ *If you suspect that a person is going to dominate the interview, set out simple ground rules before the session begins. Say something like: "We will be asking you questions for the first 45 minutes. You will be able to make your case or ask questions at the end. Is this understood?"*

Concluding the interview

❝ *My last job was decided in part on how the interview ended. They gave me a chance to ask questions and tell them why I would be the right person for the job. Then each interviewer shook me by the hand and two of them showed me back to reception. I felt very good about the company.* ❞
– Walter Stiglitz, graphic design manager

Ending an interview is just as important as opening it. It gives an important last impression which sticks in the mind of the candidate.

❝ *I'm not very good at ending interviews. Usually we run out of time, I panic and stop the discussion short, shake hands and hastily see the candidate out. It's all a bit awkward.* ❞
– Bill Samuel

Bill has just described a classically bad way to end an interview. Time-keeping is a key skill of interviewing. You should allot the same amount of time for each candidate and stick rigidly to the schedule. To do otherwise could mean the candidates' travel arrangements are jeopardised, or other appointments missed. Worse, it keeps the rest of the candidates hanging around which does nothing for the atmosphere of the interviews.

Here are some tips for ending the interview well

❑ *Stick to the timetable set so you will be able to wind things up comfortably. Build in an allowance for overruns.*

❑ *Ask the candidates if they have any further questions or comments about their suitability for the post. Ask them, if offered the job, would they accept.*

□ *Tell them what is going to happen next – especially if there is anything further they should do.*
□ *Tell them when a decision will be made and how they will hear about it.*
□ *Tell them what happens if they are unsuccessful – will their names be kept on file? What happens to portfolio work sent in? Will they get reasons why they were unsuccessful? Can they discuss the choice made with the interviewer? Emphasise that if not selected, it is no personal slight.*
□ *Ask them if they think you have covered everything.*
□ *Show them out and make sure everyone is polite and pleasant. Thank them sincerely for attending.*

The last point is very important. As you know yourself, going to an interview, even an internal one, can be a real ordeal – being thanked for facing it makes it easier for candidates to "come down".

How to make sure it goes right on the day

1. Before the interview begins, double-check that the candidates have been sent all the information they need. Also, agree with your colleagues a set of criteria against which the candidates will be rated.
2. Fit the room layout to the mood of the interview – e.g., with a chair in front of the panel for formal interview or set out in a circle for discussions.
3. Begin by welcoming the interviewee. Show them into the room yourself and establish a rapport with a little small-talk. Try to find areas of mutual interest to put the candidate at ease.
4. Start the session with a quick introduction to reinforce what you have told the candidate in advance and get the other members of the panel to introduce themselves.
5. Ensure you have your objectives straight – i.e. what information you want to get from the candidate – and that you have a strict timetable to follow. Give your interviewees plenty of opportunities to ask questions or to make their case.

6. Use all your observational powers to get to know the real candidate – as well as listening carefully to the answers, watch the body language.

7. Be prepared to deal with compulsive talkers or the terminally shy by being assertive and switching between closed and open questions.

8. Tell them what will happen next. Reassure them that if they fail to be appointed it is no slur on them. As you began, so lead them out of the room with a courteous smile and thanks.

9. Afterwards, discuss your assessment of their strengths and weaknesses with colleagues. Always double check any evidence that comes before you.

Be prepared to offer advice on where they could improve their interview skills. If you are really feeling brave, you could always ask an interviewee to assess your interviewing skills. Few have tried this but you would certainly learn a lot.

What's in this chapter for you

Why use questions? That's the question
Closed questions and open questions
Probing questions
Other useful types of questions
Ten tried and tested questions to open up the real person

> " *Do you need questions? "Most of my interview time*
> *is taken up with my questions and the interviewee's answer"*
> *"Questioning – isn't that what an interview's all about?" "I just*
> *think up questions as we go along.* "
> **– comments from experienced interviewers**

Why use questions? That's the question

There is no doubt that to most people an interview is a question
and answer session. The interviewer, the interrogator; the
candidate, the "victim". But it isn't always like that. An interview
can also be a structured and directed discussion. Some of the
best interviews have very few questions in them.

Here are some powerful alternatives to the standard question
and answer session.

- ○ *"Tell me about yourself."*
- ○ *"I would like to hear your views about our company strategy and direction."*
- ○ *"Give me an example of where you think you could drive this department forward."*
- ○ *"Let's work together on ideas to improve our customer service."*

These "discussion leads" are what you might introduce in any
brainstorming session. Why treat the interviewee any differently?
They are designed to open up discussion and free the interviewee
from the formal interrogation scenario.

> " *Actually I don't ask questions at interview.*
> *I invite ideas and discussion.* "
> **– Sandra Grevely, head of PR agency**

Despite what Sandra says, most interviewers feel the need to ask questions. The problem here is that people often don't think carefully enough about the questions they ask. Laziness can lead you into the bad habit of asking pointless questions off the top of your head. It is essential to know what you are trying to achieve with your questions. Your questions should:

○ *Elicit information*
○ *Encourage the candidate to talk*
○ *Find out what you need to know about the person's abilities, personality and skills.*

So, what is it that you need to know? Interview questions tend to cover five main areas of interest to the organisation.

○ *Is the person capable of doing the job?*
○ *Can the person fit into the existing team?*
○ *Will the person contribute to (or hinder) the development of the organisation?*
○ *Will the person accept the terms and conditions of employment?*
○ *Will the person become a reliable, long-term employee?*

Think about the questions you ask at interviews. Make sure that you know why you are asking them. Will they give you the answers to the five questions above?

Remember: questions must have a point. Think before you ask.

Closed and open questions

Good interviewers ask the right questions. This is a skill that you can improve upon quite quickly.

Are you good at asking the right questions? Once you start thinking about this, you are already on the path to becoming a better interviewer.

Different types of question have different functions. There are two main categories:

Closed questions

These questions require only a "yes" or "no" or "don't know" answer. Any question that gives a simple, short, often one-word answer, is a closed question. Here are some examples of closed questions:

- *"Did you work for Millers?"*
- *"Do you know what we do?"*
- *"How many years have you been working there?"*

Closed questions are useful for finding out the facts, but remember that you should have gleaned the "hard" information before the interview. They can also be used to rein in a chatterbox who seems incapable of giving succinct answers.

Open questions

These are designed to get the candidate talking. They invite longer answers and encourage discussion. Open questions often begin with: why, who, how, what, when. They may also begin with a "discussion leader", such as "Tell me about your ideas for improving our inventory." Here are some other examples of open questions:

- *"How did you reach your current position?"*
- *"Why did you introduce that product?"*
- *"How do you hope to move this company forward?"*

As you can see, open questions are much broader and invite a much longer answer than closed ones.

Never let the interview descend into a series of closed questions. Use them sparingly to elicit any information that wasn't made clear in the application forms. You should also use them to check facts.

Probing questions

These are used to get further into a candidate's thoughts, opinions, needs and wants. They often follow on from open questions. Here are some examples:

○ **Open question:** *"Why did you leave your last post?"*
   Probing question: *"Didn't you feel that by staying you could improve the situation?"*
○ **Open question:** *"Why do you want this job?"*
   Probing question: *"What would you say if I said that you weren't sufficiently experienced for it?"*

Probing questions are more personal, go into greater depth, and may involve an emotional response from the interviewee. They need to be carefully thought out and asked in a way that does not upset, insult or intrude unnecessarily into a person's sensibilities.

> List some closed, open and probing questions to ask an imaginary (or real) interviewee, preferably one who interviewed badly. The more you practice these, the better.

Other useful types of questions

There are other types of questions you can ask to help you control the interview and guarantee you get the details you want.

Checkers

These are questions you can ask to make sure you have understood or followed the line of argument. These often begin with:

○ *"So, to summarise, what you are saying is . . ."* or
○ *"Am I correct in assuming that . . .?"* or
○ *"What I understand you to say is . . ."*

Hypotheticals

These questions encourage the candidates to imagine themselves in a scenario of your creation. Putting them in a "work situation" can be helpful for assessing whether they are team players. For examples:

- ○ *"Imagine that, after three years in this post, you were put in charge of a major new investment project, how would you manage it . . .?"* or the classic
- ○ *"Where do you see yourself five years from now?"*

Ten tried and tested questions to open up the real person

We can't give you a set of questions that will do for all occasions but the ones here show you how to formulate good, open and probing questions which help you to make a fair judgement about the person sitting in front of you.

Consider how you can use these questions as models for your next interview

1. Tell me about a situation where your work was praised (or criticised).
2. How would you ensure that members of your team were fully motivated and working together?
3. What aspects of your current post do you dislike most? What have you done to improve the situation?
4. How do others see you?
5. What is it about this organisation that makes you want to work here?
6. What do you believe you can contribute to this organisation?
7. What would you like to be doing in three years' time?
8. What are your greatest strengths or weaknesses?
9. What would you do if you strongly disagreed with the strategy of the organisation?
10. Have we answered all of the questions you had for us?

These questions are all designed to get the interviewees to open up. They also are open-ended enough to let them develop a line of thought. They give you the chance to see them working at a problem. You may have to give them little signposts on the way if they run out of ideas. The last question is essential. As we keep saying, interviewing is a two-way process. You must give interviewees the chance to find out about you too.

Golden rules of questioning

1. Use a variety of styles and types of questions to drive the interview towards supplying the answers you need.
2. Minimise the number of closed questions. You should already have the basic information before the start of the interview.
3. Encourage the candidate to talk by asking open and hypothetical questions – i.e. questions starting with: what, when, how, why.
4. Use checkers now and again to confirm that you have understood clearly what the interviewees have said.
5. Avoid leading questions – those whose answers are inevitable and really tell you nothing new. Here are some examples: "Wouldn't you say that marketing is the most important factor in increasing profitability?" or "What do you think of people who always do the bare minimum?"
6. Also avoid long, complex questions that are very difficult for the interviewee to follow. For example, if you ask: "Why has our business gone through hard times do you think and what can be done to alleviate market conditions? How would you handle a downturn in the market share, especially given the current state of the business cycle?" the most likely response is: "Sorry, could you repeat that."
7. Keep your questions as short and simple as possible.

The only question now remaining is: "When are you going to put all these great ideas into practice?" You should now have picked up more than enough good ideas to conduct a successful interview. It takes practice, but you will now be on the road to becoming a skilful and, above all, professional interviewer. Good Luck!